Air Fryer Cookbook

The Only Air Fryer Cookbook You Will Ever Need

DIANA WATSON

Copyright © 2018 Diana Watson

All rights reserved.

Table of Contents

Introduction

Chapter 1: Mastering the Air Fryer

Chapter 2: Air Fryer Breakfast Recipes

Chapter 3: Air Fryer Lunch Recipes

Chapter 4: Air Fryer Dinner Recipes

Chapter 5: Air Fryer Dessert Recipes

Chapter 6: Air Fryer Appetizers and Snacks

Conclusion

VIP Subscriber List

Hi Dear Reader, this is Diana! If you like my book and you want to receive the latest tips and tricks on cooking, weight-loss, cookbook recipes and more, do subscribe to my mailing list in the link below! I will then be able to send you the most up-to-date information about my upcoming books and promotions as well! Thank you for supporting my work and happy reading!

Subscriber Form

http://bit.do/dianawatson

Introduction

Congratulations on purchasing the *Air Fryer Cookbook Mastery: Your Ultimate Air Fryer Recipe Book For Quick, Easy, And Healthy Foods* and thank you for doing so.

The following chapters will discuss many of the ways you can enjoy your fast-paced lifestyle, remain healthy, and take much less time to prepare your meals. All of the recipes are written in as much detail as possible so you can assemble the ingredients needed before it is time to begin the duty of breakfast, lunch or dinner.

You will discover how easy it is to make dishes from *Salmon Patties* to *Marshmallow and Yam Hand Pies* in so much less time!

There are plenty of books on this subject on the market; thanks again for choosing this one! Every effort was made to ensure it is full of as much useful information as possible. Please enjoy!

Chapter 1: Mastering the Air Fryer

How to Use the Air Fryer

The Air Fryer provides you with a way to eat healthier by providing you healthier ways to prepare your recipes without losing the texture and flavor of your homemade meals and snacks. From *French toast sticks* to *air fried ravioli* or that plateful of *Mozzarella sticks* you have been craving; you will enjoy every morsel as you learn how to prepare the recipes provided in this book.

Useful Guidelines for Recipe Measurement

With so many recipes in circulation for the air fryer (AF) provided greatly due to the Internet; you may begin to notice the many different ways they are written. This is because they travel worldwide and the best ones become viral.

These are some of the conversion tables that will guide you through the process:

- Celsius to Fahrenheit
- Grams to Cups
- Grams to Pounds
- Milliliters to Cups

Other abbreviations can include the following:

- Cup = C.
- Tablespoon = Tbsp. = T.
- Teaspoon = tsp. = t.

Going by the 'rule-of-thumb,' a handful should be between 1/3 cup to ½ cup (more or less). You might also hear a smidge or a pinch which is usually ¼ teaspoon or a dollop is usually a heaping tablespoon.

Tips for Using the Air Fryer

Tip #1: Many pre-made packaged food items you already purchase can be cooked using the Air Fryer. Each food may vary with its cooking time. As a guideline, reduce the cooking times by about 70% compared to times in a conventional oven.

Tip #2: While cooking smaller items such as fries or wings; you can make sure they are cooking evenly by shaking the basket several times during the cooking process.

Tip #3: It is important to pat food items dry if you have marinated or soaked them in to help eliminate splattering or excessive smoke.

Tip #4: It is tempting when you are in a rush to attempt to overload the Air fryer. Don't put too much in the cooking basket at one time. You won't receive the best results if the air cannot make the 360° turns that make the cooker so unique.

Tip #5: Allow at least three minutes warm-up time each time you use the fryer so it can reach its correct starting temperature.

Tip #6: When it comes time to clean the cooking basket, loosen any food particles remaining attached to the basket. Soak each of the attachments in a soapy water solution before scrubbing or placing it in the dishwasher.

Tip #7: If you use aluminum foil or parchment paper, leave a one-half-inch space around the bottom edge of the basket.

Tip #8: Cooking sprays are an excellent choice to spray on your food before cooking. You can also spray the mesh of the cooking basket to keep anything from sticking to its surface.

Proof You Should Own an Air Fryer

Benefit #1: It is a beginner's treat. You can locate your favorite recipes and whip up a remarkable meal at home in half of the time. The machine does the hard work for you. All you need to do is program the temperature and times.

Benefit #2: The Fryer Needs Less Oil: It won't be necessary to add oil to the cooker if you have frozen products which are meant for baking. You only need to adjust the timer and cook. All of the excess fat will drip away into a tray beneath the basket.

You can cook whatever meats you enjoy and receive delicious and healthy results. You will understand this once you begin trying out some of these new recipes.

For example; you can cook French fries with a tablespoon of oil versus a vat of oil.

Benefit #3: No Oily Clean Up: You only need to remove the cooking bowl, drip pan, or the cooking basket. It is inside a cover which means you won't have oil vapor deposits on the walls, floors, or countertops.

You can use the dishwasher to clean the movable parts. You can also use a sponge to clean the bits of food that might be stuck to the AF surfaces.

Benefit #4: Purchase Less Oil: It is possible to splurge on the more expensive oils since you only use such a minimal amount.

Benefit #5: Multitasking Features: The Air Fryer is capable of functioning as so many products, whether you need an oven, a hot grill, a toaster, a skillet, or a deep fryer—it is your answer! It can be used for breakfast, lunch, dinner, desserts, and even snacks.

Benefit #6: Safety Functions: The machine will automatically shut down when the cooking time is completed. You will have less burned or overheated food items.

The unit will not slip because of the non-slip feet which help eliminate the risk of the machine from falling off of the countertop. The closed cooking system helps prevent burns from hot oil or other foods.

Now that you know how to avoid some of the pitfalls you may have with your new Air Fryer unit; you can begin planning which delicious treat you want to test first!

Chapter 2: Air Fryer Breakfast Recipes

Apple Dumplings

Ingredients

2 Tbsp. raisins

2 small apples (peeled—cored)

1 Tbsp. brown sugar

2 sheets puff pastry

2 Tbsp. melted butter

Instructions

1) Preheat the Air Fryer to 356°F.
2) Mix the sugar and raisins.
3) Place each apple on one of the pastry sheets and fill with the raisins/sugar.
4) Fold the pastry over until the apple and raisins are fully covered.
5) Place them on a piece of foil so they cannot fall through the fryer.
6) Thoroughly brush them with the melted butter.
7) Set the timer for 25 minutes. It is ready when the apples are sold and browned.

Note: Be sure to use very small apples for this yummy treat.

Banana Fritters

Ingredients

8 ripe peeled bananas

3 Tbsp. corn flour

One egg white

3 Tbsp. vegetable oil

¾ cup breadcrumbs

Instructions

1) Preheat the fryer at 356°F.
2) In a skillet using the low heat setting; pour the oil and toss in the breadcrumbs, cooking until golden brown.
3) Use the flour to coat the bananas; dip them into the egg white, and coat them with the bread crumbs.
4) Place the bananas on a single layer of the basket and air fry for eight minutes.
5) Remove and sit on paper towels.

What a delicious treat to be served warm!

Tip: If you have too many breadcrumbs; you can place them in the fridge in an airtight container to use sometime in the future.

French Toast Sticks

Ingredients

2 gently beaten eggs

4 slices of desired bread

2 tablespoons soft margarine or butter

Cinnamon

Salt

Ground cloves

Nutmeg

Garnish: Maple syrup

Instructions

1) Preheat the Air Fryer to 356°F.
2) Whisk the eggs, a shake of nutmeg, cloves, and cinnamon together in a small bowl.
3) Spread butter on both sides of the bread, and cut them into strips.
4) Dredge each of the cuts in the egg mix, and arrange in the fryer. (You will need to make two batches.)
5) Pause the fryer after two minutes, remove the pan, and spray the bread with cooking spray.
6) Flip and spray the other side, returning them to the AF for an additional four minutes, making sure they do not burn.
7) It's ready when it is golden brown; serve them immediately.

Garnish with some maple syrup or whipped cream.

Yields: Two Servings

Bacon and Eggs

Ingredients

4 eggs

12 (1/2-inch thick) slices of bacon

Pepper and salt

1 Tablespoon butter

2 sliced croissants

4 Tablespoons softened butter

BBQ Sauce Ingredients

1 C. ketchup

¼ C. apple cider vinegar

2 Tablespoons each:

- Brown sugar

- Molasses

½ teaspoon each:

- Onion powder

- Mustard powder

1 Tablespoon Worcestershire sauce

½ teaspoon liquid smoke

Instructions

1) Preset the temperature in the Air Fryer to 390°F.

2) On the stovetop, using medium heat—mix the molasses, ketchup, brown sugar, vinegar, onion powder, and mustard power using a small saucepot. Whisk the liquid smoke and

Worcestershire sauce into the mixture to blend thoroughly. Cook until the sauce thickens. Add additional flavoring as desired.

3) Place the bacon on the trays and cook for five minutes. Remove and brush the bacon with the barbecue sauce –flip— and brush the other side—return to the cooker and continue cooking another five minutes.

4) Butter the halved croissant and toast it in the fryer.

5) In the meantime, use a non-stick pan using the med-low setting on the stovetop—melt the butter. Add four eggs to the pan, cooking until the white starts setting—flip and cook about thirty more seconds.

6) Remove from the pan, and enjoy with the bacon and croissant.

Yields: Four Servings

Cheesy Mushroom, Ham, and Egg

Ingredients

3 slices honey shaved ham

1 croissant

4 halved cherry tomatoes

4 small quartered button mushrooms

1 egg

1.8 ounces mozzarella or cheddar cheese

Optional: ½ roughly chopped rosemary sprig

Instructions

1) Lightly grease a baking dish with butter to prevent the mixture from sticking.
2) Preset the Air Fryer to 320°F.
3) Place the ingredients on 2 layers with cheese in the center and top layer.
4) Make a space in the center of the ham and crack the egg.
5) Sprinkle the rosemary and a smidgen of salt and pepper for flavoring over the mixture.
6) Put it into the preheated basket for eight minutes. Take the croissant out of the AF after four minutes to allow more time for the egg to cook.

Yields: One Serving

Scrambled Eggs

Ingredients

2 eggs

Pepper and salt to taste

Instructions

1) Preset the Air Fryer to 284°F for about five minutes.
2) Put the butter in the fryer to melt, and spread it out evenly.
3) Empty the eggs and any other ingredients such as cheese or tomatoes.
4) Open the AF every few minutes to whisk to the desired yellow and fluffy consistency.

Make a scrambled egg sandwich or with toast on the side.

Air Fryer Spinach Frittata

For a fantastic meal good for breakfast, lunch, dinnertime, or anytime; you have found it!

Ingredients

1/3 package (or so) of spinach

1 small minced red onion

Mozzarella cheese

3 eggs

Instructions

1) Preset the Air Fryer at 356°F for at least three minutes.
2) Add oil to a baking pan for one minute.
3) Add the onions and continue cooking for two to three minutes; toss in the spinach and cook three to five minutes additional minutes.
4) Whisk in the eggs, add the seasonings, cheese, and add to the pan.

5) Cook for eight minutes. Season with salt and pepper.

Bacon Wrapped Tater Tots

Ingredients

3 tablespoons sour cream

1 pound sliced bacon (medium)

1 large bag crispy tater tots

4 scallions

½ cup shredded cheddar cheese

Instructions

1) Preheat the Air Fryer to 400°F.
2) Wrap each of the tots in bacon and place them into the fryer basket. Don't overcrowd, keep them in a single layer.
3) Set the AF timer for 8 minutes.
4) When the timer beeps; place the tots on a plate.
5) Serve with the scallions and cheese garnish. Add a dash of sour cream and enjoy.

Yields: Four Servings

Buttermilk Biscuits

These have to be considered for breakfast also because they are so delicious!

Ingredients

½ C. cake flour

¾ tsp. salt

1-¼ C. all-purpose flour

¼ tsp. baking soda

1 teaspoon granulated sugar

½ tsp. baking powder

¾ C. buttermilk

4 Tbsp. unsalted cold butter (cut into cubes) + melt 1 Tbsp.

Optional for Serving:

Honey or preserves

Butter

Note: Additional flour is needed for dusting the counter or cutting board.

Instructions

1) Preheat the Air Fryer to 400°F.
1) Sift together the all-purpose flour, sugar, cake flour, baking soda, and the salt in a medium mixing dish.

2) Use a pastry cutter (or your fingers) to blend the ingredients into pea-sized consistency. Pour in the buttermilk and stir using a rubber spatula (or your hands), and make a dough ball. Try not to over-mix the dough.

3) Sprinkle some flour on the counter surface and begin to press the dough into about a ½-inch thickness. It should be approximately eight inches in diameter.

4) Use a cutter to cut the dough into biscuits; dip the tip of the tip of the cutter with the flour making a swift cut. If you twist the dough; it could prevent it from rising.

5) Place the biscuits in a pan and brush them with the melted butter. Place the dough in the basket of the fryer and set the timer for eight minutes.

Enjoy the finished product with some honey or your favorite preserves, jam, or jelly.

Vegan Mini Bacon Wrapped Burritos

Ingredients

2 servings Tofu Scramble or Vegan Egg

2-3 tablespoons tamari

2 tablespoons cashew butter

1-2 tablespoons water

1-2 tablespoons liquid smoke

4 pieces of rice paper

Vegetable Add-Ins

8 strips roasted red pepper

1/3 cup sweet potato roasted cubes

1 small sautéed tree broccoli

Handful of greens (kale, spinach, etc.)

6-8 stalks of fresh asparagus

Instructions

1) Line the pan used for baking with parchment. Preheat the Air Fryer to 350°F.

2) Whisk the tamari, cashew butter, water, and liquid smoke; set to the side.

3) Prepare the fillings.

4) Hold a rice paper under cool running water—getting both sides wet—just a second. Place on the plate to fill.

5) Start by filling the ingredients –just-off- from the center— leaving the sides of the paper free.

6) Fold in two of the sides as you would when you make a burrito. Seal them and dip each one in the liquid smoke mixture—coating completely.

7) Cook until crispy; usually about eight to ten minutes.

Yields: Four Mini Burritos

DIANA WATSON

Chapter 3: Lunch Recipes

Grilled Cheese Sandwich

Ingredients

½ Cup sharp cheddar cheese

4 Slices white bread or brioche

¼ Cup melted butter

Instructions

1) Pre-set the Air Fryer temperature to 360°F.

2) Spread butter on each side of all of the bread slices, and put the cheese on two of them; putting them together. Cook until browned, about five to seven minutes.

Yields: Serves Two

Cheeseburger Mini Sliders

Ingredients

6 Slices cheddar cheese

1 Pound ground beef

6 Dinner Rolls

Black pepper and Salt

Instructions

1) Pre-set the heat on the Air Fryer to 390°F.

2) Form 6 (2 ½-ounce) patties and flavor with the pepper and

salt

3) Place the burgers on the AF basket for ten minutes.

4) Take them from the cooker and add the cheese; returning to the Air Fryer for an additional minute until the cheese melts. Yummy!

Yields: Serves Three

Pigs In A Blanket

Ingredients

1 (Eight-ounce) Can crescent rolls

1 (Twelve-ounce) Package cocktail franks

Instructions

1) Preheat the Air Fryer to 330°F.

2) Drain the franks and thoroughly dry them using two paper towels.

3) Slice the dough into strips of about 1 ½ inches x 1-inch (rectangular).

4) Roll the dough around the franks leaving the ends open. Put them in the freezer to firm-up for about five minutes.

5) Take them out, and put them in the AF for six to eight minutes. Adjust the temperature to 390°F, and continue to

cook for approximately three minutes.

Yields: Serves Four

Chicken

AF Chicken 'Fried'

Ingredients

2 chicken thighs (skinless)

3 sprigs fresh parsley

Garlic powder (to dust the thighs)

Salt and black pepper if desired

½ a lemon

Chili flakes as you like

1 to 2 sprigs fresh rosemary

Instructions

1) Rinse the thighs. Drain them between two paper towels. (Discard the towels and wash your hands.)
2) Clean the rosemary sprigs and remove the stems. Chop or mince the parsley.

3) *For the Marinate:* Combine the salt and pepper, garlic powder, rosemary leaves, parsley, chili flakes, and lemon juice. Add the thighs and marinate overnight in the refrigerator.

4) *Preheat the Air Fryer:* Set the AF to 356°F.

5) Grill for 12 minutes.

Note: Times may vary depending on the thickness/size of the thighs.

AF Buffalo Chicken Wings

Ingredients

5 chicken wings (about 14 ounces)

½ teaspoon garlic powder (optional)

2 teaspoons cayenne pepper

2 tablespoons red hot sauce

1 tablespoon (15 grams) melted butter

Fresh black pepper and salt to taste

Instructions

1) Preheat the Air Fryer at 356°F.
2) Cut the wings into three sections (the end tip, mid joint, and drumstick). Pat each one thoroughly dry using a paper towel. Wash your wash right away to prevent cross contamination.
3) Combine a dash of pepper and salt, the garlic powder, and cayenne pepper in a plate. Lightly coat the wings with the powder.
4) Place the chicken on the wire rack and back for 15 minutes; turning once at 7 minutes.

5) Combine the hot sauce, and melted butter in a dish to garnish the baked chicken when it is time to be served.

Notes: Save and freeze the end tip for preparing chicken stock.

You can increase the cayenne pepper if you want it hotter.

Country Style Chicken Tenders

Ingredients

¾ pounds chicken tenders

2 tablespoons olive oil

½ teaspoon salt

2 beaten eggs

½ cup all-purpose flour

½ cup seasoned breadcrumbs

1 teaspoon black pepper

Instructions

1) Preheat the Air Fryer heat to 330°F.
2) Set up three separate dishes for the flour, eggs, and breadcrumbs.

3) Blend the salt, pepper and bread crumbs. Four in the oil with the breadcrumbs and mix. Put the chicken tenders into the flour, and the eggs. Coat evenly with the breadcrumbs. Shake the excess off before placing in the Air Fryer basket.

4) Cook for ten minutes at 330°F and increase to 390°F for five minutes or until they are a nice golden brown.

Chinese Chicken Wings

Ingredients

4 chicken wings

Salt and pepper to taste

1 tablespoon each:

- Chinese spice
- Mixed spice
- Soy sauce

Instructions

Preheat the AF to 180°C/356°F.

1) Add the seasonings into a large mixing container—stirring thoroughly.

2) Blend the seasonings over the chicken wings until each piece is covered.

3) Put some aluminum foil on the base of the AF (similar to how you cover a baking tray), and add the chicken sprinkling any remnants over the chicken. Cook for 15 minutes.

4) Flip the chicken and cook another 15 minutes at 200C/392F.

Yields: Two Servings

Chicken Pot Pie

Ingredients

6 chicken tenders

2 potatoes

1 ½ cups condensed cream of celery soup

¾ cup heavy cream

1 thyme sprig

1 whole dried bay leaf

5 refrigerated buttermilk biscuits (dough)

1 tablespoon milk

1 egg yolk

Instructions

1) Preheat the Air Fryer at 320°F.

2) Peel and dice the potatoes.

3) Mix all of the ingredients in a pan except for the milk, egg yolk, and biscuits. Bring them to a boil using medium heat.

4) Empty the mixture into the baking tin and use some aluminum foil to cover the top. Place the pan into the fry basket. Set the timer for 15 minutes.

5) Meanwhile, after the pie completes the cycle make an egg wash with the milk and egg yolk. Place the biscuits on the baking pan and brush with the egg wash mixture.

6) Set the timer to 300°F for an additional ten minutes.

7) Your pie is ready when the biscuits are golden brown.

Yields: Four Servings

Tarragon Chicken

Ingredients

1 skinless and boneless chicken breast

⅛ Teaspoon fresh ground black pepper

½ Teaspoon unsalted butter

⅛ Teaspoon kosher salt

¼ Cup dried tarragon

Instructions

1) Pre-set the cooker to 390°F.
2) Cut a piece of heavy-duty aluminum foil—approximately 12 x 12 or you can double a regular strength one and fold in half. Put the chicken on it.
3) Place the butter and tarragon on top of the chicken and flavor with pepper and salt—loosely wrapping the chicken for minimal airflow.
4) Cook for 12 minutes in the Air Fryer basket, remove the meal from the wrapper and enjoy.

Beef

Beef Roll Ups

Ingredients

6 slices provolone cheese

2 pounds beef flank steak

3 tablespoons pesto

¾ cup fresh baby spinach

1 teaspoon each sea salt and ground black pepper

3-ounces roasted red bell peppers

Instructions

1) Preheat the Air Fryer cooker to 400°F.
2) Open the steak up and add the butter and pesto evenly on the meat.
3) Layer in the spinach, peppers, and cheese about three-quarters the way down through the meat.
4) Roll the mixture and secure it with toothpicks or skewers.
5) Set the timer for 14 minutes; flipping the beef halfway through the cooking process.

6) Let the meat rest for a minimum of ten minutes before attempting to cut and serve the tasty delight.

Yields: Four Servings

Air Fried Ravioli

Ingredients

1 package meat or cheese ravioli

1 jar Marinara sauce

2 C. breadcrumbs (Italian-style)

1 C. buttermilk

¼ C. Parmesan cheese

Olive oil

Note: Purchase the sauce and ravioli ready-made.

Instructions

1) Preheat the Air Fryer to 200°F.
2) Empty the buttermilk into a container and dip the ravioli.
3) Put a spoonful of oil to the breadcrumbs. Coat the ravioli with the crumbs.
4) Add the ravioli into the AF on baking paper for around five minutes.

Roasted Veggie Pasta Salad

Ingredients

4 ounces brown mushrooms

1 red onion

1 yellow squash

1 zucchini

1 each bell peppers

- Red
- Green
- Orange

Pinch of Fresh ground pepper and salt

1 teaspoon Italian seasoning

1 cup grape tomatoes

½ cup pitted Kalamata olives

1 pound cooked Rigatoni or Penne Rigate

¼ cup olive oil

2 tablespoons fresh chopped basil

3 tablespoons balsamic vinegar

Instructions

1) Cut the squash and zucchini into half-moons. Cut the peppers into large chunks and slice the red onion. Slice the tomatoes and olives in half.

2) Preheat the Air Fryer to 380°F.

3) Put the mushrooms, peppers, red onion, squash, and zucchini in a large container.

4) Drizzle with some of the oil—tossing well. Sprinkle in the pepper, salt, and Italian seasoning.

5) Place in the Air Fryer until the veggies are soft (not mushy), usually about for 12 to 15 minutes. For even roasting; shake the basket about halfway through the cooking cycle.

6) Combine the roasted veggies, olives, cooked pasta, and tomatoes, in a large container; mix well. Add the vinegar, and toss. (Use as little oil as possible, just enough to coat the vegetables.)

7) Keep it refrigerated until ready to serve—adding the fresh basil for last.

Yields: Six to Eight Servings

Chapter 4: Air Fryer Dinner Recipes

Chicken and Turkey Recipes

Lemon Rosemary Chicken

Ingredients

1 pound chicken (350 g)

For the Marinate:

1 tablespoon soy sauce

½ tablespoon olive oil

1 teaspoon minced ginger

For the Sauce:

3 tablespoons brown sugar

1 tablespoon oyster sauce

½ wedge-cut lemon in skins

Optional: 15 g (0.5 ounces) fresh rosemary

Instructions

1) Leave the skin on the rosemary and chop.

2) Blend all of the marinade components. Pour over the chicken. Let them cool off in the fridge for about thirty minutes.

3) Place the marinade and chicken in a baking dish, and bake for six minutes in the AF at 392°F.

4) Blend all of the sauce ingredients (minus the lemon).

5) Pour the mixture over the chicken when it is about half baked.

6) Place the lemon wedges in the pan evenly and squeeze so the zest will heighten the flavor of the chicken. Continue baking for an additional 13 minutes turning to ensure all of the pieces are browned evenly.

Note: You can omit the rosemary.

Jamaican Chicken Meatballs

Ingredients

1 large peeled and diced onion

2 large chicken breasts

1 teaspoon chili powder

2 tablespoons honey

Pepper and salt to taste

3 tablespoons soy sauce

1 tablespoon each

- Dry mustard
- Cumin
- Thyme
- Basil

Optional: 2 teaspoons Jerk Paste

Instructions

1) Using a blender—mince the chicken; add the onion and mince; mix well. Toss in the Jamaican seasonings and blend again. Make ten medium balls.
2) Place on the baking mat in the AF and cook at 356°F or 180°C.
3) Put them on a stick when done cooking and some use of the extra sauce over the meatballs.
4) Add several herbs on the top, serve, and enjoy.

Yields: Ten Servings

Note: In case you are not aware; jerk paste is a combination of brown spices, ginger, peppers, and thyme.

Roast Turkey Breast

Ingredients

1 tablespoon ground black pepper

8 pounds bone-in turkey breast

2 tablespoon each:

- Olive oil
- Sea salt

Instructions

1) Preheat the Air Fryer on 360°F.
2) Rub the turkey with olive oil and flavor with the seasonings.
3) Put the turkey in the preheated basket for 20 minutes.
4) When done, flip it over and adjust the cooking time for another 20 minutes (also at 360°F).
5) The breast of turkey is done when it registers 165°F when thermometer tested.
6) Allow the meat rest a minimum of 20 minutes before serving.

Spicy Rolled Meat

Ingredients

1 (1.6 pounds/500 g) turkey breast fillet

½ tsp. chili powder

1 ½ tsp. ground cumin

1 crushed garlic clove

1 tsp. cinnamon

2 Tbsp. olive oil

1 small finely chopped onion

2 Tbsp. flat-leafed parsley (finely chopped)

Needed: Rolled meat String

Instructions

1) Preset the heat on the Air Fryer at 356°F/180°C.
2) Put the meat onto a cutting board with the short end facing you. Cut the full length of the fillet. Stop cutting about (2 cm, 13/16inches) from the edge and about 1/3 of the way from the top. Fold this section open and cut it again from this side and open the meat.
3) Combine the cinnamon, chili powder, 1 teaspoon of salt, pepper, and cumin in a mixing container in a small mixing container. Pour in the oil.
4) Spoon one tablespoon of the mixture into a small dish and add the parsley and onion.
5) Use the mixture to coat the meat.
6) Tie it starting at 1 ¼-inch intervals.
7) Rub the outside with the herbal mixture for about 40 minutes or until nicely browned.

Yields: Four Servings

Fish and Seafood

Salmon Patties

Ingredients

1 salmon portion (about 7 ounces)

3 large russet potatoes (about 14 ounces)

1/3 cup frozen veggies (parboiled & drained)

2 dill sprinkles

Dash of salt and pepper

1 egg

Coating: breadcrumbs

Olive oil spray

Instructions

1) Set the Air Fryer to 356°F.
2) Peel and chop the potatoes into small bits and boil for about ten minutes.
3) Mash and place in the fridge to chill.
4) Grill the salmon for five minutes, flake it apart and set it to the side.
5) Combine all of the ingredients and shape into patties.
6) Evenly coat with the breadcrumbs, and spray them with a bit of olive spray.
7) Place in the Air Fryer for ten to twelve minutes.

Yields: Six to Eight Patties

Dill Salmon

Ingredients for the Salmon

4 (6-ounce pieces) or 1 ½ pounds salmon

1 Pinch of salt

2 Teaspoons olive oil

Ingredients for the Dill Sauce

½ cup each:

- Sour cream
- Non-fat Greek yogurt
- 2 (finely chopped) tablespoons dill
- 1 Pinch of salt

Instructions

1) Preheat the AF to 270°F.
2) Slice the salmon into the four portions, and drizzle with half of the oil (1 teaspoon). Flavor with a pinch of salt and add to the basket for about 20 to 23 minutes
3) *Make the Sauce.* Blend the sour cream, yogurt, salt, and dill in a mixing container. Pour the sauce over the cooked salmon as a garnish with a pinch of the chopped dill.

Yields: Serves Four

Halibut Steak With a Teriyaki Glazed Sauce

Ingredients

1 Lb. halibut steak

Ingredients for the Marinade

½ cup mirin (Japanese cooking wine)

2/3 cup low-sodium soy sauce

¼ cup sugar

¼ cup orange juice

2 tablespoons lime juice

¼ teaspoon each:

- Ground ginger
- Crushed red pepper flakes

1 smashed garlic clove

Instructions

1) Preheat the Air Fryer to 390°F.
2) Combine all of the marinade ingredients in a saucepan, bring it to a boil and reduce to medium heat; cool.

3) Pour half of the marinade in a resealable plastic bag with the halibut. Chill in the fridge for thirty minutes.

4) Cook the halibut for ten to twelve minutes. Brush some of the remaining glaze over the steak.

5) Serve over top a bed of rice. Add a little basil or mint for some extra jazz.

Yields: Serves Three

Cajun Shrimp

Ingredients

1 tablespoon olive oil

½ teaspoon Old Bay seasoning

16 to 20 (1 ¼ pounds) tiger shrimp

¼ teaspoon each:

- smoked paprika
- cayenne pepper

1 pinch of salt

Instructions

1) Preheat the Air Fryer to 390°F.

2) Mix all of the ingredients and coat the shrimp with the oil and spices.

3) Place the shrimp into the basket and cook for five minutes.

4) Complement the meal with some rice and place the shrimp on top for a tasty luncheon treat.

Coconut Shrimp

Ingredients

12 Large raw shrimp

1 tablespoon cornstarch

½ tablespoon oil

1 Cup each:

- Raw egg whites
- Unsweetened dried coconut
- White all-purpose flour
- Panko

Instructions

1) Drain the shrimp on towels

2) Preheat the AF to 350°F.

3) Combine the coconut and panko in a container and set it to the side; blend the cornstarch and oil in another dish.

4) Put the egg whites into another container, and a third one for the coconut mix.

5) Cover each shrimp in the cornstarch mix, the egg whites, and lastly the coconut mixture.

6) Cook for ten minutes; flipping them after five minutes for even cooking.

Yields: Three Servings

Beef

Rib Steak

Ingredients

1 Tablespoon of steak rub

2 pounds rib steaks

1 Tablespoon of olive oil

Instructions

1) Before it is time to cook; preheat the Air Fryer to 400°F.

2) Flavor the meat on all areas with the oil and rub.

3) Put it in the basket for 14 minutes, flipping after seven minutes.

4) Let it rest for at least ten minutes before you slice and serve.

Yields: Two Servings

Stromboli

Ingredients

1 (12-ounce) refrigerated pizza crust

¾ cup Mozzarella shredded cheese

3 cups shredded cheddar cheese

1 tablespoon milk

1 egg yolk

1/3 pound sliced cooked ham

3 ounces roasted red bell peppers

Instructions

1) Preheat the Air Fryer at 360°F.

2) Roll the dough until it is around ¼-inch thick.

3) Layer in the peppers, ham, and cheese on one side of the dough and fold to seal.

4) Combine the milk and eggs to brush the dough.

5) Put the Stromboli in the basket and set the timer for 15 minutes. Check it every five minutes or so—flip the Stromboli to the other side for thorough cooking.

Yields: Four Servings

Roasted Rack of Lamb with a Macadamia Crust

Ingredients

1 clove of garlic

1 Tbsp. olive oil

Pepper and salt

1 ¾ pounds - rack of lamb

Ingredients for the Crust

3 ounces Macadamia nuts (unsalted)

1 tablespoon each

- Fresh rosemary
- Breadcrumbs

1 egg

Instructions

1) Preheat the Air Fryer to 220°F.

2) Chop the garlic clove into tiny bits. Make the garlic oil by combining the garlic and oil. Brush the lamb and flavor with salt and pepper.

3) Chop the nuts to a fine consistency in a bowl and blend in the rosemary and breadcrumbs. Beat/whip the egg in another dish.

4) Dredge the meat through the egg mixture and coat with the macadamia crust topping.

5) Place the rack of lamb in the Air Fryer basket—setting the timer for 30 minutes.

6) After the time is lapsed; raise the heat to 390°F—setting the time for an additional five minutes.

7) Take the meat from the fryer and let it rest for about ten minutes covered with some aluminum foil.

Substitutes: You can use cashews, hazelnuts, pistachios, or almonds if you would like a change of pace.

Crispy Tofu

Ingredients

2 tsp. toasted sesame oil

2 Tbsp. soy sauce

1 tsp. seasoned rice vinegar

1 block firm pressed tofu

1 tablespoon cornstarch or potato starch

Instructions

1) Cut the tofu into 1-inch cubes. Preheat the Air Fryer to 370°F.

2) In a shallow dish, mix the vinegar, soy sauce, oil, and tofu. Let the combination marinate for 15 to 30 minutes. Toss the marinated product with the cornstarch and add it to the AF basket.

3) Cook for 20 minutes, shaking the basket halfway through the cooking cycle.

Yields: Four Servings

Sides

Bread Rolls with Potato Stuffing

Ingredients

8 slices bread (white part only)

5 large potatoes

1 small bunch finely chopped coriander

2 seeded and finely chopped green chilies

½ teaspoon turmeric

2 curry leaf sprigs

½ teaspoon mustard seeds

2 finely chopped small onions

2 tablespoons oil (frying and brushing)

Salt if desired

Instructions

1) Preheat the Air Fryer to 392°F.

2) Cut away the edges of the bread.

3) Peel the potatoes, and boil. Use one teaspoon of salt, and mash the potatoes.

4) In the meantime, on the stovetop use a skillet to combine the mustard seeds and one teaspoon of the oil. Add the onions when the seeds sputter, continue frying until they become translucent. Toss in the curry and turmeric.

5) Fry the mixture a few seconds, then add the salt, mashed potatoes; mix well, and let it cool.

6) Shape eight portions of the mixture into an oval shape. Set to the side.

7) Wet the bread with water, and press it into your palm to remove the excess water.

8) Place the oval potato into the bread and roll the bread completely around the potato mixture. Be sure they are completely sealed.

9) Brush the basket and the potato rolls with oil, and set to the side.

10) Set the Air Fryer timer for 12 to 13 minutes. Let them cook until crispy and browned.

Yields: Four Servings

Avocado Fries

Ingredients

1 large avocado

Pinch of black pepper and salt

¼ teaspoon paprika or cayenne pepper

¼ cup all-purpose flour

½ cup Panko breadcrumbs

1 beaten egg

¼ of a lemon

Instructions

1) Preheat the Air Fryer to 392°F.

2) Cut the avocado into eight slices.

3) Using three separate containers; add the salt, cayenne, pepper, and flour in one. Place the beaten egg in the second one and breadcrumbs in the third one.

4) Coat the avocado with the flour, egg, and breadcrumbs.

5) Put the avocado into the fryer basket and set the timer for six minutes.

6) They will be golden in color when ready to serve.

Enjoy with some Greek yogurt and honey or with a squeeze of fresh lemon juice.

Broccoli

Ingredients

2 Lbs. broccoli crowns

2 Tablespoons olive oil

1 teaspoon kosher salt

½ teaspoon black pepper

2 teaspoons grated lemon zest

1/3 cup Kalamata olives

¼ cup shaved Parmesan cheese

Instructions

1) Remove the stems from the broccoli and cut them into 1 to 1-1/2- inch florets. Pit and cut the olives in half.

2) Over high heat, fill a medium pan with six cups of water—bring it to boiling. Toss in the florets and cook for three to four minutes. Remove and drain. Add the pepper, salt, and oil

3) Set the AF to 400°F.

4) Place the broccoli into the basket, close the drawer, and click the timer for 15 minutes. Toss/flip at seven minutes for even browning. When done, place the broccoli in the bowl.

5) Garnish with lemon zest, olives, and cheese. Enjoy immediately.

Yields: Two to Four Servings

Fact: The Kalamata olive is a native of southern Greece which is often times preserved in olive oil or wine vinegar. It is an additional 'kick' for this treat!

Buffalo Cauliflower

Ingredients

1 cup breadcrumbs

4 cups cauliflower florets

¼ cup buffalo sauce

¼ cup melted butter

For the Dip: Your favorite dressing

Instructions

1) Place the butter in a microwaveable dish; remove and whisk in the buffalo sauce.

2) Dip each of the florets in the buttery mixture; the stem does not need to have sauce. Use the stem as a handle, hold it over a cup and let the excess drip away.

3) Run the floret through the breadcrumbs to your liking. Drop them into the fryer. Cook for 14 to 17 minutes at 350°F. (The unit will not need to preheat since it is calculated in the time.)

4) You can shake the basket several times to be sure it is evenly browning. Enjoy with your favorite dip, but be sure to eat it right away because the crunchiness goes away quickly.

Note: Reheat in the oven. Don't reheat it in the microwave; it will be mushy.

Yields: Four Servings

Cheesy Potatoes

Ingredients

7 medium potatoes

½ cup grated Gruyere (semi-mature) cheese

½ cup cream

½ cup milk

1 teaspoon black pepper

½ teaspoon nutmeg

Instructions

1) Peel and slice the potatoes wafer-thin. Russet potatoes work great with this recipe.
2) Preset the Air Fryer to 400°F.
3) Blend the milk and cream; add the nutmeg, pepper, and salt for seasoning.
4) Generously coat the potatoes with the mixture.
5) Put the slices in an 8 x 8 dish, pouring the rest of the mixture over the potatoes.
6) Place the dish into Air Fryer and set the timer for 25 minutes.
7) Remove the dish and sprinkle the cheese over the hot potatoes.
8) Continue cooking until the cheese is melted and browned, usually an additional ten minutes.

Yields: Serves Six

French Fried Potatoes

Ingredients

6 medium peeled potatoes

2 Tbsp. olive oil

Instructions

1) Preheat the Air Fryer to 360°F.

2) Peel and cut the potatoes into 3-inch strips x ¼-inch.

3) Soak the cut potatoes for a minimum of thirty minutes in water, and drain thoroughly. Pat them dry with a towel.

4) Coat the potatoes with the oil in a large mixing container.

5) Dropthe potatoes into the cooking basket for about thirty minutes or until they are the desired doneness.

6) Shake the basket two or three times during the cooking phase.

Note: The time may vary depending on the thickness of the potatoes.

Potatoes au Gratin

Ingredients

7 Medium peeled russet potatoes

½ cup each:

- Cream
- Milk

½ teaspoon nutmeg

1 teaspoon black pepper

½ cup semi-mature (Gruyere) grated cheese

Instructions

1) Preheat the Air Fryer to 390°F.
2) Wash and slice the potatoes wafer-thin.
3) Blend together the cream and milk—flavoring with some pepper, salt, and nutmeg.
4) Use the milk mixture to coat the potatoes.
5) Place the slices into an eight-inch baking pan/dish and pour the remainder of the milk/cream mixture on top of the potatoes.
6) Place the heat-resistant dish onto the cooking basket—setting the timer for 25 minutes.
7) Take the basket out and sprinkle with the cheese.
8) Bake ten more minutes or until

browned.

Note: You can use two eggs instead of milk.

Yields: Six Servings

Homemade AF Croutons

Try these with a healthy salad:

Ingredients

Stale Bread

Butter

Optional: Olive oil

Instructions

1) Preheat the Air Fryer for about two to three minutes at 248°F. (You can always adjust the time but don't hotter than 320°F.)
2) Cube some of the old bread to the sizes you want to use for your meal. Pour in the olive oil and melted butter.
3) Put the cubed bread into the basket and cook for two to three minutes.
4) Toss and cook for an additional two to three minutes.
5) Completely cool and keep in an airtight container for no more than two days.

Portobello Mushrooms

Ingredients

1.4 Oz. cubed ham (about two slices)

4 Tbsp. extra virgin olive oil

7.05 Oz. Portobello mushrooms

2 shiitake or button mushrooms

1.8 Oz. Mozzarella cheese (shredded)

1 Tbsp. chopped garlic

Optional: Ground black pepper and salt

Instructions

1) Preheat the AF cooker at 356°F.
2) Clean, cap, and remove the stalks from the mushrooms; use a couple of paper towels to pat them dry.
3) Use 1/2 of the oil to brush the Portobello mushrooms tops and place them cap side down on a baking tray lined with aluminum foil or parchment paper.
4) Divide the mushrooms and top with cheese, garlic, the other half of mushrooms—diced, and the cubed ham.
5) Flavor with the pepper and salt. Drizzle a bit of the oil over the mushrooms.
6) Cook for about 10 minutes. Garnish with some dried or fresh parsley.

The Blooming Onion

Ingredients

4 small/medium onions

4 dollops of butter

1 Tbsp. olive oil

Instructions

1) Peel the skin from the onion and cut away the top and bottom to reveal flat ends.
2) Soak the onions in salt water for four hours to take away the harshness.
3) You'll need to cut the onion as far down as you can without severing the onion. Cut four times to make eight segments.
4) Preheat the fryer to 350°F.
5) Put the onions in the fryer and drizzle with the oil—placing a dollop of butter on each one.
6) Cook in the AF until the outside is dark, usually about thirty minutes.

Note: 4 dollops is 4 heaping tablespoons

Yields: Four Servings

Onion Rings

Ingredients

For a side dish or quick snack; purchase four ounces of frozen, battered onion rings.

Instructions

1) Preheat the Air Fryer cooker to 360°F.
2) Place the frozen onion rings in the basket for ten minutes.
3) Take them from the cooker and give them a toss.
4) Reset the timer for an additional ten minutes or more if needed.

Fat-Free Fries

Ingredients

1 to 2 sweet potatoes

1 to 2 red potatoes

Sprinkle of pepper and salt

Cooking spray

Optional: Parsley

Instructions

1) Preset the Air Fryer for 356°F.
2) Peel and cut the potatoes; place in a container of water until ready for frying.
3) Use two layers of paper towels to dry the wedges and spray them with the oil.
4) Place a single layer of fries in the basket and set the timer for ten minutes.
5) After the time is up, give the fries a shake, return to the AF for an additional eight to ten minutes.

6) Take them from the fryer and season as you wish.

Garnish with a bit of parsley.

Potato Croquets

Ingredients

7 small cubed red potatoes

1 egg yolk

2 Tablespoons all-purpose flour

½ cup grated Parmesan cheese

1 Pinch Each:

- Cayenne
- Black pepper
- Salt

For the Breading:

1 cup all-purpose flour

2 Tablespoons vegetable oil

2 beaten eggs

½ cup panko

1 Pinch of nutmeg

Instructions

1) Preset the temperature on the Air Fryer to 390°F.

2) In salted water, boil the potatoes for 15 minutes, drain, and mash. Cool completely.

3) Add the flour, cheese, and egg yolk—flavoring with nutmeg, pepper, and salt,

4) Shape the filling into golf ball size.

5) Make a crumbly mixture of the breadcrumbs and oil. Put each ball into the flour mixture, the eggs, and then the panko. Roll them into cylinder shapes.

6) Put them in the cooking basket until browned—about seven to eight minutes.

Yields: It will probably take 2 batches depending on how large you made the balls.

Potato Skin Wedges

Ingredients

6 medium russet potatoes

1 ½ tsp. paprika

½ tsp. salt

2 Tbsp. canola oil

½ tsp. black pepper

Instructions

1) Thoroughly wash the potatoes under the tap. Boil the potatoes in salted water about forty minutes.
2) Cool in the refrigerator for about thirty minutes. Quarter them when cooled.
3) Combine the paprika, pepper, salt, and oil in a mixing dish. Toss the potatoes in the mixture.
4) Place in the cooking basket with the skin side down. Cook them until golden brown; about 14 to 16 minutes.

Grilled Tomatoes AF Style

Ingredients

2 tomatoes

Cooking spray

Pepper

Herbs

Instructions

1) Preheat the fryer to 320°F.
2) Wash and cut the tomatoes into halves. Spray each of them lightly with some cooking spray and place them cut side facing upwards. Sprinkle with your favorite spices—fresh or dried—including the pepper, sage, rosemary, basil, oregano, and any others of your choice.

3) Put them into the basket for 20 minutes or until they are to the doneness you want to achieve. If they are ready to enjoy—if not—cook for a few more minutes.

This would be tasty breakfast or as a side dish.

Yields: Two Servings

Chapter 5: Air Fryer Desserts

Blackberry Apricot Crumble

Ingredients

5 ½ ounces fresh blackberries

2 tablespoons lemon juice

18 ounces fresh apricots

½ cup sugar

Pinch of salt

1 cup flour

5 tablespoons cold butter

Instructions

1) Preheat the Air Fryer to 390°F.

2) Prepare an eight-inch oven dish with a small amount of cooking oil.

3) Remove the stones, cut the apricots into cubes, and place them in a container.

4) Mix the lemon juice, blackberries, and 2 tablespoons of sugar with the apricots and mix. Place the fruit in the oven dish.

5) Combine a pinch of salt, the remainder of the sugar, and the flour in a mixing container. Add 1 tablespoon cold water and the butter; using your fingertips to make a crumbly mixture.
6) Sprinkle the crumbles over the fruit and press down.
7) Place the dish into the basket and slide it into the Air Fryer for 20 minutes. It is ready when it is cooked thoroughly, and the top is browned

Cheesecake: Lemon Ricotta

Ingredients

1 lemon

$2/3$ cups (150g) sugar

2 cups (500g) ricotta

2 teaspoons vanilla essence

Instructions

1) Zest and juice the lemon.
2) Preset the Air Fryer to 320°F.
3) Mix the sugar, ricotta, 1 tablespoon lemon juice as well as the zest, and the vanilla essence—stirring until fully mixed. Blend in the cornstarch and pour into the oven dish.
4) Place the dish in the Air Fryer basket and set the timer for 25 minutes.
5) The middle should be set when the cake is complexly done.

6) Leave the cheesecake on a wire rack to fully cool.

Cherry Pie

Ingredients

2 refrigerated pre-made pie crusts

1 Can cherry pie filling (21-ounces)

1 tablespoon milk

1 egg yolk

Instructions

1) Preheat the fryer to 310°F.
2) Stab holes into the crust after placing into a pie plate. Allow the excess to hang over the edges. Place in the AF for five minutes
3) Take the basket out and set the crust on the counter. Fill it with the cherries. Remove the excess crust.
4) Cut the remainder crust into ¾-inch strips placing them as a lattice across the pie.
5) Make an egg wash with the milk and egg; brush the pie.
6) Bake for fifteen minutes.
7) Serve with the ice cream of your choice.

Yields: Eight Servings

Donut Bread Pudding

Ingredients

6 glazed donuts

4 raw egg yolks

1 ½ cups whipping cream

¼ cup sugar

¾ cup frozen sweet cherries

1 teaspoon cinnamon

½ cup semi-sweet chocolate baking chips

½ cup raisins

Instructions

1) Preheat the fryer at 310°F.
2) Combine the wet ingredients in a container and combine the rest of the ingredients and mix.
3) Pour into a baking pan and cover it with foil. Place it into the basket and set the timer for 60 minutes.
4) Chill the bread pudding well before serving.

Yields: Four Servings

Fluffy Peanut Butter Marshmallow Turnovers

Ingredients

4 defrosted sheets filo pastry

4 Tbsp. chunky peanut butter

2-ounces melted butter

4 tsp. marshmallow fluff

A Pinch of sea salt

Instructions

1) Preset the temperature of the Air Fryer to 360°F.
2) Use the melted butter to brush one sheet of the filo. Put the second sheet on top and brush it also with butter.
3) Continue the process until you have completed all four sheets.
4) Cut the layers into four (4) 12-inch x 3-inch strips.
5) Place one teaspoon of the marshmallow fluff on the underside and 1 tablespoon of the peanut butter.
6) Fold the tip over the filo strip to form a triangle, making sure the filling is completely wrapped.
7) Seal the ends with a small amount of butter. Place the completed turnovers into the AF for three to five minutes.
8) When done, they will be fluffy and golden brown.
9) Add a touch of sea salt for the sweet/salty combo.

Notes: The Filo/Phyllo pastry is a little different than regular pastry. It is tissue thin and has very little fat content. It is considered okay by some bakers and is interchange the filo with regular puff pastry for turnovers.

Yields: Four Servings

Marshmallow and Yam Hand Pies

Ingredients

1 crescent dough sheet

1 (16-ounce can) candied yams

1/2 teaspoon cinnamon

1/4 teaspoon allspice

2 tablespoons marshmallow crème

1/4 teaspoon salt

1 egg, beaten

For the Maple Glaze:

1/2 cup maple syrup

½ cup confectioners' sugar

Instructions

1) Pre-set the heat on the AF to 400°F.
2) Drain the syrup from the yams. Combine the cinnamon, salt, allspice, and yams using a fork to the blend the spices and smash the yams.
3) Put the dough sheet onto a board and cut into four equal sections.
4) Spoon the filling onto the squares and add a tablespoon of the crème.

5) Use a brush to spread the egg over the edges of the dough and place the remainder of the two pieces of dough on top of the pies.

6) Use a fork to crimp the edges and cut three slits into the top for venting.

7) Place in the Air Fryer for six minutes.

8) Make the glaze from the sugar and syrup in a small dish—slowly adding the syrup—until the sugar dissolves.

9) To serve, drizzle the glaze over the warm pies and enjoy.

Yields: Four Servings.

Orange and Pineapple Fondant

Ingredients

4.2 ounces (115) g Butter

4.2 ounces (115 g) Dark chocolate

2 medium eggs

4 tablespoons castor sugar (see note below)

2 tablespoons self-rising flour

1 medium orange (rind and juice)

Instructions

1) Grease four ramekins with a small amount of oil or cooking spray.
2) Pre-set the heat in the Air Fryer to 356°F/380°C.
3) Cut and tear apart the orange and grate the orange peel.
4) Melt the butter and chocolate in a double boiler or in a glass measuring cup over a pot of hot water. Stir until it is creamy smooth.
5) Beat and whisk in the sugar and eggs—until frothy and pale. Blend in the sugar and egg mixture along with the orange bits. Add the flour and mix until well-blended.
6) Fill the ramekins about ¾ of the way full with the mixture. Cook in the Air Fryer for 12 minutes.
7) Take it from the fryer and let them rest for two minutes. (They will continue to cook.) Turn them out of the containers (upside down) into a serving platter. You can loosen the edges by tapping the ramekin gently with a butter knife.
8) The fondant will release from the center to provide you with a luscious center of pudding.
9) Garnish with some caramel sauce or vanilla ice cream.

Yields: Four Servings

How to Make Castor Sugar

Castor or caster sugar is simply granulated sugar that has been placed into a blender or food processor to make it a 'super-fine' sugar used for some recipes since it melts easier.

Instructions

1) Put the granulated sugar into the blender/food processor.
2) Pulse until it is a 'super-fine' texture—not powdery.

Pineapple Sticks with Yogurt Dip

Ingredients

¼ C. desiccated (moisture-free) coconut

1 C. vanilla yogurt

1 small sprig fresh mint

Instructions

1) Preheat the Air Fryer to 392°F.
2) Meanwhile, use similar shapes and sizes to cut the pineapple into sticks.
3) Dip the sticks into the coconut. Place the pineapple sticks in the basket and cook for ten minutes
4) *For the Dip*: Dice the mint into the yogurt.

Yields: Four Servings

Strawberry Cupcakes and Strawberry Icing

Ingredients

½ cup castor sugar

½ cup butter

2 medium eggs

½ cup self-rising flour

½ cup butter

½ teaspoon vanilla essence

½ cup icing sugar

1 tablespoon whipped cream

½ teaspoon pink food coloring

¼ cup fresh (blended) strawberries

Instructions

1) Set the Air Fryer temperature to 338°F/170°C.
2) Cream the sugar and butter in a large mixing container until it is creamy smooth.
3) Add the eggs one at a time along with the vanilla essence.
4) Blend in a small amount of flour at a time until all is completely mixed.
5) Pour them into ramekins about 80% of the way full. Place them in the Air Fryer for eight minutes.

6) *Make the Frosting:* Cream the butter and slowly mix in the icing sugar until creamy. Pour in the food coloring, (blended) strawberries, and whipped cream—mix well.

7) Take them out and use a piping bag to make the swirly frosting for a tasty 'pretty' cupcake every time.

Yields: Ten Servings

Chapter 6: Air Fryer Appetizers and Snacks

Cheesy Garlic Bread

Ingredients

5 round bread slices

5 teaspoons sun-dried tomato pesto

3 chopped garlic cloves

4 Tbsp. melted butter

1 cup grated Mozzarella cheese

Garnish Options:

- Chili flakes
- Chopped basil leaves
- oregano

Instructions

1) Preheat the Air Fryer to 356°F.
2) Cut the loaf of bread into 5 thick slices.
3) Add the butter, pesto, and cheese on the bread.
4) Put the slices in the preheated cooker for six to eight minutes.
5) Garnish with your choice of toppings.

Note: Round or Baguette bread was used for this recipe. It is recommended to add the finely chopped garlic cloves to the melted butter ahead of time for the best results.

Clams Oregano

Ingredients

2 dozen shucked clams

1 cup unseasoned breadcrumbs

4 tablespoons melted butter

3 clove minced garlic

1 teaspoon dried oregano

¼ cup chopped parsley

¼ cup grated Parmesan cheese

For the Pan:

- 1 cup sea salt

Instructions

1) Preheat the AF to 400°F.
2) Mix the oregano, parsley, parmesan cheese, breadcrumbs, and melted butter in a medium container.
3) Using a heaping tablespoon of the crumb mixture; add it to the exposed clams.
4) Fill the insert with the salt, place the clams inside and cook for three minutes.

5) Dress them up with a garnish of lemon wedges and fresh parsley.

Yields: Four Servings

Corn Tortilla Chips

Ingredients

8 corn Tortillas

1 Tbsp. olive oil

Salt if desired

Instructions

1) Preset the AF to 392°F.
2) Use a sharp knife to cut the tortillas.
3) Brush each tortilla with oil.
4) Air fry two batches for three minutes each. Sprinkle with a pinch of salt.

Crab Sticks

Ingredients

1 package 'DoDo' crab sticks

Cooking spray

Instructions

1) Take each of the sticks out of the package; find an edge, and unroll until flat.
2) Tear the sheets into 1/3 widths.

3) Place them on a plate and coat them with cooking spray.

4) Cook them in the AF for 10 minutes.

5) *Note*: If you shred the crab meat; you can cut the time in half, but they will also easily fall through the holes in the basket.

Garlic Knots

Ingredients

Marinara sauce

1 teaspoon sea salt

1 Lb. frozen pizza crust dough

1 tablespoon each:

- Garlic powder
- Grated Parmesan cheese
- Fresh chopped parsley

Instructions

1) Preheat the Air Fryer to 360°F.

2) Roll out the dough until is about 1 ½ to 2-inches thick. Slice it approximately ¾-inches apart—lengthwise.

3) Roll the dough and make it into knots.

4) Add the cheese, oil, and spices in a bowl, and roll each knot in the mixture before placing it into the fry basket.

5) Set the timer for 12 minutes; flipping halfway through the cooking process (six minutes).

Serve with a dish of marinara sauce.

Yields: Four Servings

Kale Chips

Ingredients

1 Tbsp. olive oil

1 head of kale

1 tsp. Soya sauce

Instructions

1) De-stem the kale and tear it into 1 1/2 –inch pieces.
2) Rinse in cold water and thoroughly dry using some paper towels.
3) Toss the kale with the soya sauce and oil.
4) Set the Air Fryer for 200°F for two to three minutes; toss when half cooked.

Meatballs for the Party

Ingredients

2 ½ Tablespoons Worcestershire sauce

1 pound ground beef

1 Tablespoon Tabasco

¾ cup tomato ketchup

1 Tablespoon lemon juice

¼ cup vinegar

½ teaspoon dry mustard

½ cup brown sugar

3 crushed gingersnaps

Instructions

1) Combine all of the seasonings in a large mixing container—blending well.
2) Mix the beef and continue churning the ingredients.
3) Make the balls and put them in the fryer. Cook on 375°F for 15 minutes.
4) Place them on the toothpicks before serving.

Note: They are ready when the center is done, and they are crispy.

Yields: 24 Servings

Feta Triangles

Ingredients

4 ounces feta cheese

1 egg yolk

2 tablespoons finely chopped flat-leafed parsley

2 sheets frozen (defrosted) filo pastry

1 finely chopped scallion

2 tablespoons olive oil

Ground black pepper

Instructions

1) Pre-set the heat in the Air Fryer to 390°F.
2) Whisk the egg and blend in the scallion, feta, and parsley.
3) Cut the dough into three strips.
4) Place a heaping teaspoon of the feta mix underneath the pastry strip.
5) Fold the tip to form a triangle as you work your way around the strip.
6) Use a small amount of oil and brush each of the triangles before placing them in the cooker basket cooking them for three minutes.
7) Lower the heat to 360°F, and continue cooking for an additional two minutes.

Yields: Five Servings

Mozzarella Sticks

Ingredients

2 eggs

1 pound or block Mozzarella cheese

1 cup plain breadcrumbs

¼ cup white flour

3 tablespoons nonfat milk

Instructions

1) Preheat the fryer to 400°F.
2) Slice the cheese into ½-inch x 3-inch sticks.
3) Whisk the milk and egg together in one bowl, with the oil and bread crumbs in individual dishes as well.
4) Dredge the sliced cheese through the oil, egg, and breadcrumbs.
5) Place the sticks on bread tin and put them in the freezer compartment for about an hour or two.
6) Place them in small increments (don't overcrowd) into the AF basket.
7) Cook for 12 minutes.

Yields: Four Servings

Mini Quiche Wedges

Ingredients

1 (3 ½ ounces or 100 g) Frozen or ready-made pizza crust

1 egg

(1.4 ounces or 40 g) Grated cheese

½ tablespoon oil

3 tablespoons whipping cream

Fresh ground pepper

2 small pie molds

Instructions

1) Pre-set the heat on the Air Fryer to 392°F/200°C.
2) Use a bit of cooking spray to grease the molds. Line them with the dough pressing down around the edges.
3) Whisk the cheese, cream, and egg flavoring with some pepper and salt to taste. Empty the mixture into the molds.
4) Put the mold into the basket and set the timer for 12 minutes. Bake the second one the same way.
5) Take them from the molds and slice each of the quiche into six wedges.
6) You can serve at room temperature or warm.

Try these Variations:

Ingredients for Mushroom Slices

4.4 ounces or 125 g sliced mushrooms

1 teaspoon paprika

1 crushed clove of garlic

OR

Ingredients Ham and Broccoli

1.8 ounces or 50 g small broccoli florets and ham

Instructions for Ham and Broccoli

Boil the florets until tender.

Divide between each of the quiches.

Yields: Nine Servings

Spicy Pumpkin Patch Cannoli Treats for Halloween

Ingredients

4 tablespoons melted butter

8 large flour tortillas

1 cup sugar

½ cup orange sanding sugar

2 pounds whole milk ricotta

1 tablespoon ground cinnamon

2/3 cup confectioners' sugar

1 ½ cup pumpkin pie mix

½ cup mini chocolate chips

Instructions

1) Preheat the Air Fryer for three minutes at 400°F.
2) Use a pumpkin cookie cutter to make the tortillas.
3) Brush one side of the cutouts with the butter and sprinkle them with the orange sanding sugar.

4) Mix the cinnamon a regular sugar in a small dish; sprinkle over the cookies.
5) Bake the treats in batches until crispy (about three minutes).
6) Use wire racks for cooling.
7) Make the dip by using a large bowl and combining the cinnamon sugar, pumpkin pie, mix, and ricotta in a large mixing dish. Stir well.
8) Be creative and place the dip in a shallow serving platter.
9) Place the crisps into the dip to make a pumpkin patch and decorate with the chips.

Yields: Four Servings

Sweet Potato Chips

Ingredients

2 Large Sweet potatoes

1 Tbsp. olive oil

Instructions

1) Pre-set the heat in the Air Fryer to 350°F
2) Peel and slice the potatoes into chips. It is best to slice them into the same sizes so then will cook evenly.

3) Place the potatoes into a resealable baggie and add the oil. Shake the potatoes to coat them completely.

4) Pour the sweet potatoes into the Air Fryer and cook for approximately fifteen minutes, depending on the thickness.

Index

Chapter 2: Breakfast Recipes

- Apple Dumplings

- Banana Fritters

- French Toast Sticks

- Bacon and Eggs

- Cheesy Mushroom, Ham, and Egg

- Scrambled Eggs

- Air Fryer Spinach Frittata

- Bacon Wrapped Tater Tots

- Buttermilk Biscuits

- Vegan Mini Bacon Wrapped Burritos

Chapter 3: Lunch Recipes

- Grilled Cheese Sandwich
- Cheeseburger Mini Sliders
- Pigs In A Blanket

Chicken

- AF Chicken 'Fried'
- AF Buffalo Chicken Wings
- Chinese Chicken Wings
- Country Style Chicken Tenders
- Chicken Pot Pie
- Tarragon Chicken

Beef

- Beef Roll Ups
- Air Fried Ravioli
- Roasted Veggie Pasta Salad

Chapter 4: Dinner Recipes

Chicken and Turkey Recipes

- Lemon Rosemary Chicken
- Jamaican Chicken Meatballs
- Roast Turkey Breast
- Spicy Rolled Meat

Fish and Seafood

- Salmon Patties
- Dill Salmon
- Halibut Steak With a Teriyaki Glazed Sauce
- Cajun Shrimp
- Coconut Shrimp

Beef

- Rib Steak
- Stromboli
- Roasted Rack of Lamb with a Macadamia Crust

- Crispy Tofu

Sides

- Bread Rolls with Potato Stuffing
- Avocado Fries
- Broccoli
- Buffalo Cauliflower
- Cheesy Potatoes
- French Fried Potatoes
- Potatoes au Gratin
- Homemade AF Croutons
- Portobello Mushrooms
- The Blooming Onion
- Onion Rings
- Fat-Free Fries
- Potato Croquets
- Potato Skin Wedges
- Grilled Tomatoes AF Style

Chapter 5: Air Fryer Desserts

- Blackberry Apricot Crumble
- Cheesecake: Lemon Ricotta
- Cherry Pie
- Donut Bread Pudding
- Fluffy Peanut Butter Marshmallow Turnovers
- Marshmallow and Yam Hand Pies
- Orange and Chocolate Fondant
- Pineapple Sticks with Yogurt Dip

Chapter 6: Air Fryer Appetizers and Snacks

- Cheesy Garlic Bread
- Clams Oregano
- Corn Tortilla Chips
- Crab Sticks
- Garlic Knots
- Kale Chips
- Meatballs for the Party
- Feta Triangles

- Mozzarella Sticks

- Mini Quiche Wedges

- Spicy Pumpkin Patch Cannoli Treats for Halloween

- Sweet Potato Chips

Copyright © 2018 Diana Watson

All rights reserved.

Table of Contents

Introduction

Chapter 1: What is a Spiralizer?

Chapter 2: Ways to Utilize a Spiralizer

Chapter 3: 4-Ingredient Creamy Vodka Steak Pasta

Chapter 4: 20 Minute Healthy Chicken Parmesan

Chapter 5: Rainbow Vegetarian Pad Thai with Peanuts and Basil

Chapter 6: 15 Minute Spicy Shrimp with Pesto Noodles

Chapter 7: Creamy Spinach Sweet Potato Noodles with Cashew Sauce

Chapter 8: Low Carb Zucchini Pasta

Chapter 9: Squash Zoodler Omelet

Chapter 10: Spiralized Apple Salad

Chapter 11: Spiralized Carrot and Radish Salad with Peach Vinaigrette

Chapter 12: Baked Mexican Chips in a Stick

Conclusion

What IS a spiralizer?

If you have no idea what a spiralizer is, you are not alone. There are many individuals that either come across spiralizer recipes online or see one in an appliance store and wonder what the heck it is and how they would even go about using it if they were to purchase one. These devices are more commonly seen within the kitchens of big restaurants, but it is becoming a more and more popular kitchen gadget that regular people just like you are utilizing in their very own home kitchens to create unique dishes.

Spiralizers are often used to substitute pasta in main dishes, using vegetables instead of typical pasta. What does this mean for you? Well, it could mean MUCH healthier eating, as well as getting your particularly picky children to eat their veggies without them knowing. Ten points for parenting skills! Spiralizers are also amazing tools to use if you have loads of chopping of slicing to complete for bigger sized portions, such as get-togethers and whatnot.

Ways to Utilize a Spiralizer

If you are a newcomer to this kitchen device, then you may have no inkling on how to actually use it in your own kitchen. The two main points on a spiralizer is the round circle covered in spikes with the handle attached and the opposite side that assists in holding what you want to spiralize. To some, it may look like quite like an estranged piece of equipment that some child whipped together for a science project. But it does get the job done! You can spiralize just about any sort of vegetable and even fruit, as long as it is of the hard variety. If you try to spiralize mushy foods, it will turn into a total pile of wet mush. And no one wants to eat that. Cut off the stems of whatever you want to put through this gadget, peel if necessary and put the smaller end of the food at hand around the round hole at the top of the metal blades. You need the whole to be positioned within the middle of the vegetable and ensure that it is straight as possible. Press down upon the base of the spiralizer as you crank the handle.

There are many things you can create with the help of a spiralizer. Cute, functional and fun to look at spirals can be made from just about anything you can dream up! Some of the main foods that people who own one of these babies spiralize are:

- Zucchini

- Bell Peppers
- Apples
- Sweet Potatoes
- Cucumbers
- Cabbage
- Red Onions
- Yellow Squash

The main concept that went behind the making of this invention was being able to substitute veggies for pasta, instead of filling our bodies with loads of carbs from noodles, making your own noodles made out of vegetables is a much healthier alternative, especially if you are in the market to lose a bit of weight. It's quite the no-brainer!

Like I said, the possibilities are pretty endless! It takes some practice, creativity, and just plain experimenting when it comes to utilizing your spiralizer! Remember those cool Play-Dough contraptions you had growing up? The spiralizer is kind of like that, but you are making REAL food you can eat, in a fun way!

The remainder of this book is filled with recipes that you can try and make for you and your family in the comfort of your own home! Do not be afraid to get others involved. Bonding in the kitchen is a tradition and the spiralizer is a great way to get your children interested in how you make their favorite dishes!

4-Ingredient Creamy Vodka Steak Pasta

What's in it:

- 2-3 large zucchini
- 35-40 ounces of DeLallo Vodka Sauce
- 1 pound sirloin steak
- 2 tbsp. butter

How it's made:

- Get a heavy skillet and heat it to a medium-high temperature. Afterwards, heat up butter until lightly browned but not black
- Cut steak in bite sized pieces and turn up skillet heat higher. Add steak to skillet and let sit without disturbing it for at least 1 minute. Flip pieces of steak over and cook for 1-2 minutes until both sides are seared.
- Remove steak from skillet and put in a bowl.
- Wipe out skillet with a paper towel to remove grease. Add sauce to skillet. Pour in pieces of steak and let simmer in sauce for 5-10 minutes
- While steak is simmering, spiralize zucchini into noodles
- Top noodles with meat sauce
- Serve with sprinkled parmesan cheese and parsley if desired.

20 Minute Healthy Chicken Parmesan

What's in it:

- 2 zucchinis
- 1 tsp. Italian herbs
- 4 slices of fresh mozzarella cheese
- 1 ½ c. DeLallo Creamy Vodka tomato sauce
- 4 chicken breasts
- 2 tbsp. oil
- ¼ c. Parmesan cheese
- ¼ c. panko bread crumbs
- ¼ c. whole wheat breadcrumbs
- Salt/pepper as you prefer

How it's made:

- Ensure your oven is preheated to 425 degrees
- In a shallow dish, toss together Parmesan cheese, panko, and breadcrumbs along with Italian herbs salt and pepper.
- Get a skillet and warm it to about a medium-high temperature. Afterward, warm the oil in the skillet.
- Cut the chicken breasts into four pieces
- Dredge chicken in breadcrumbs and add to skillet, frying each side for 3-4 minutes until browned.
- Put the skillet in the over and bake for 5-10 minutes until chicken is cooked. Add sauce and slice of mozzarella and then place back inside over until cheese is bubbling and lightly brown in color
- Spiralize zucchini as chicken finishes cooking to create noodles. Serve alongside chicken and sprinkle generously with Parmesan cheese and parsley

Rainbow Vegetarian Pad Thai with Peanuts and Basil

What's in it:

For Pad Thai:

- ½ c. fresh herbs
- ½ c. chopped peanuts
- 1 beaten egg
- 2 tbsp. oil
- 2 carrots
- Half of a yellow onion
- 1 red pepper
- 1 zucchini
- 4 oz. brown rice noodles

For the sauce:

- 1 tsp. chili paste
- 1 tbsp. soy sauce
- 3 tbsp. chicken or veggie broth
- 3 tbsp. brown sugar
- 2 tbsp. white vinegar
- 3 tbsp. fish sauce

How it's made:

- Fill a bowl with cold water and place uncooked noodles in it to soak
- Spiralize onion, red pepper, and zucchini into noodle shapes. Then cut carrots into small pieces or spiralize them if they are big enough
- In a jar, shake up all the sauce components
- In a pan, heat up oil over medium-high heat. Pour in all veggies. Stir-fry them using tongs for around 2-3 minutes or

- until they are crisply tenderized. DO NOT OVERCOOK. Pour into another bowl and set aside.
- In same pan, add more oil, drain then add noodles, stir-frying for 1 minute, using the tongs to toss.
- Add sauce and fry for 1-2 more minutes until the sauce thickens and sticks to noodles.
- Push noodles to side of pan and pour beaten egg into the pan, letting cooking about 30 seconds. Proceed to toss everything with your pair of tongs. Eggs will stick to noodles and entire dish will become sticky in texture.
- Pour in veggies, tossing everything together and remove pan from heat.
- Mix in peanuts and herbs, enjoy!

15 minute Spicy Shrimp with Pesto Noodles

What's in it:

For Pesto:

- Juice of 1 lemon
- 2 garlic cloves
- ½ tsp. salt
- ¼ c. water
- ½ c. olive oil
- ¾ c. almonds
- 1 c. mixed basil and/or parsley
- 1 c. spinach
- 1 c. kale

For the Shrimp and Noodles:

- 4 medium zucchini
- Salt and pepper to taste
- 1 pound of shrimp
- 1 tbsp oil or butter

How it's made:

- In a food processor, pulse all pesto ingredients until smooth in texture. This should make around 2 cups of pesto. Set aside just 1 cup of pesto and utilize the rest for another recipe you desire to make.
- Get a skillet and warm it to a medium-high temperature. Afterwards, warm the oil and add in shrimp. Toss with spices.
- Sauté shrimp with spices until all are coated and fully cooked, meaning they are no longer translucent in color.
- Spiralize zucchini into noodle shapes.
- Toss zucchini noodles with pesto and top with shrimp and serve

Creamy Spinach Sweet Potato Noodles with Cashew Sauce

What's in it:

- Olive oil (to garnish)
- Fresh herbs at your discretion
- 2 c. baby spinach
- 4 spiralized large sweet potatoes
- 1 tbsp. oil
- 1 clove of garlic
- Salt/pepper as desired
- ½ tsp. of salt
- ¾ c. of water
- 1 c. of cashews

How it's made:

- In a bowl, pour in cashews and let soak in water for at least 2 hours
- Drain and rinse cashews thoroughly and pour into a food processor. Add in garlic, salt, ¾ cup of water and puree until you get a smooth textured mixture
- Grab a skillet and warm it to a high temperature. Afterwards, warm the oil.
- Add sweet potatoes and toss for around 6-7 minutes until crisply tenderized. Remove from heat and add in spinach
- Combine mixture with around half the herbs of choice, adding in water if your mixture becomes too sticky. Season as you desire.
- Drizzle with olive oil and top with remaining herbs. Enjoy!

Low Carb Zucchini Pasta

What's in it:

- Salt and Pepper to taste
- ¼ c. of water
- 1 tbsp. olive oil
- 2 peeled zucchinis

How it's made:

- Spiralize both zucchinis until they are shaped in the form of thin spaghetti
- Get a skillet and warm it to a medium-high temperature. Afterward, warm the olive oil and pour in zucchini noodles for 1 minute
- Add water and cook zucchini until it is softened, which takes about 5 to 7 minutes
- Season with salt and pepper and serve alone or alongside another entrée.

Squash Zoodler Omelet

What's in it:

- Salt and pepper to taste
- 2 tbsp. mozzarella cheese, shredded
- ¼ c. milk
- 2 eggs
- 2 tbsp. fresh cilantro, chopped
- ¼ c. fresh spinach
- 1 tbsp. butter
- 1 yellow squash

How it's made:

- Cut the ends off of yellow squash and then spiralize it to form noodles
- In a skillet over medium high heat, heat butter
- Add squash noodles, cilantro, and spinach to skillet and cook until tender, which takes around 5 to 7 minutes. Then proceed to spread mixture evenly in skillet
- In a bowl, mix together milk and eggs, then pour over squash mixture
- Cook until eggs are firm, usually takes about 5 minutes
- Pour mozzarella cheese over egg mixture and cook until cheese is melted, usually takes around 5 minutes
- Season with salt and pepper before serving. Enjoy!

Spiralized Apple Salad

What's in it:

- 1 tbsp. pine nuts
- 1 tbsp. Dijon mustard
- ½ of a lime, juiced
- 2 tbsp. extra-virgin olive oil
- 1 unpeeled red delicious apple
- 2 unpeeled granny smith apples
- 1 tsp. honey + more to taste
- 2 tbsp. white balsamic vinegar

How it's made:

- In small bowl, mix together honey, Dijon mustard, white balsamic vinegar and olive oil to make a dressing
- Spiralize both granny smith and red delicious apples
- In a large bowl, toss apple noodles with lime juice to keep them from browning.
- Pour dressing over top of apples noodles, mixing gently to combine
- Toast the pine nuts over a low heat until they are light brown.
- Sprinkle nuts over salad before enjoying

Spiralized Carrot and Radish Salad with Peach Vinaigrette

What's in it:

- 1 tsp. fresh chives
- 1 tbsp. shredded coconut
- 1 tbsp. slivered almonds
- 1/3 of a daikon radish
- 1 large carrot
- Salt and pepper to taste
- 1 pinch of garlic powder
- 1 tsp. peach-infused balsamic vinegar
- 1 tbsp. lemon-infused olive oil

How it's made:

- In a bowl, mix together pepper, salt, garlic powder, peach-infused vinegar and lemon-infused olive oil to make up the vinaigrette
- Spiralize carrots and cut them into ribbons. Toss carrot ribbons into vinaigrette and let stand until they are soft, which takes about 10 minutes
- Spiralize radishes and cut into ribbons. Toss radishes into carrot mixture.
- Sprinkle with chives, coconut, and almonds before serving

Baked Mexican Chips on a Stick

What's in it:

- 1 pinch sea salt
- 2 tsp. sriracha sauce
- 6 bamboo skewers
- 2 tsp. taco seasoning
- 2 russet potatoes
- Cooking spray

How it's made:

- Ensure oven is preheated to 425 degrees. Line a baking sheet with greased foil
- Spiralize each potato, and then cut each spiral into shorter pieces
- Thread potato spirals onto skewers
- Put skewers on baking sheet and spray with cooking spray, then sprinkle with taco seasoning
- Roast in over for 17-18 minutes
- Season with sriracha sauce and sea salt before consuming

Table of Contents

Introduction

Chapter 1: What the Mediterranean Diet Is

Chapter 2: Breakfast Recipes

Chapter 3: Lunch Recipes

Chapter 4: Dinner Recipes

Chapter 5: Continue the Plan

Conclusion

Index for Recipes

VIP Subscriber List

Hi Dear Reader, this is Diana! If you like my book and you want to receive the latest tips and tricks on cooking, weight-loss, cookbook recipes and more, do subscribe to my mailing list in the link below! I will then be able to send you the most up-to-date information about my upcoming books and promotions as well! Thank you for supporting my work and happy reading!

Subscriber Form

http://bit.do/dianawatson

Chapter 1: What The Mediterranean Diet Is

Traditional Origins of the Mediterranean Diet

During the 1960s many traditional foods became popular originating from Crete, Greece, and Southern Italy as the baseline for many of the menu plans. American researchers began to detect how these specific people had remained so much healthier in comparison to the people living in the United States.

The first to association with the Mediterranean diet was *The Seven Countries Study* which began in 1957 and has lasted for decades. The study involved Finland, Yugoslavia, the Netherlands, Japan, Italy, Greece and the United States. The initial enrollment involved 12,000 healthy middle-aged men. Ancel Keys, the main investigator, discovered the seven countries had the lowest cardiovascular disease rates, apparently because of the diet planning of those areas.

Epidemiologic studies have indicated that those that consume a more typical 'Western' diet which is rich in, dairy products, red meat as well as foods which have been artificially sweetened and contain more salt will consume less of the fish, veggies, legumes, whole grains, and fruits provided in the Mediterranean Diet.

Many of the standard American diets are focused on refined carbohydrates, fried or fast foods and many others which contain high levels of saturated or trans fats, as well as sodium. These plans lead to deficiencies in minerals, vitamins, and fiber.

Benefits of the Plan

These are just a few of the ways the Mediterranean diet plan can provide you a healthier lifestyle:

Improved Weight Loss: Individuals on the Mediterranean diet plan lost over three times more weight than those on other plans as stated by a New England Journal of Medicine.

Helps to Prevent Heart Attacks: The reduced level of oxidized low-density lipoprotein (LDL) cholesterol is evident with the plan.

Type 2 Diabetes: Better control of sugar levels/blood glucose

Helps to Prevent Strokes and Alzheimer's Disease: The reduction of blood sugar levels and general blood vessel health is improved.

Improved Moods: Over 15,000 individuals were studied in Spain and found the amounts of omega-3 fatty acids contributed to a lower risk of developing depression.

The Plan Helps to Keep Your Body More Agile: Muscle weakness and other frailty signs are reduced by as much as 70 % for those who followed the plan.

Essential Nutrients are Consumed: You probably wonder how all of this is possible with the high fat in the diet. You are less likely to be hungry with the protein, fiber, and healthy fats entering your body. The veggies will make up the volume in the meals. These types of foods will not cause a spike in blood sugar, resulting in hunger in an hour or so. You can make it through the day without all of the extra snacks.

Premature Death: Over 1.5 million healthy adults have been associated with living a fuller life on the diet plan. That calculates to a 20% reduced risk of death rate at any age.

Tips of How to Reap the Benefits

Adapting to a strict Mediterranean diet plan is best described by taking advantage of the methods used in a food pyramid of sorts. The following lists will provide essential information of how to balance the plan. These are those guidelines:

Monthly Goals: Four servings of red meat

Weekly Goals:

- Fish: Five to six servings
- Poultry: Four servings
- Nuts, olives, pulses: Three to four servings
- Eggs: Three servings
- Potatoes: Three servings
- Sweets: Three servings

Daily Goals:

- Olive Oil: The main added lipid
- Dairy Products: Two servings
- Fruit: Three servings
- Veggies: Six servings
- Non-refined cereals and Similar Products: Eight Servings: This group includes brown rice, as well as whole grain pasta and bread.

Add some physical activity to the combination and drink plenty of water. Replace some of your salt intake with herbs such as thyme, basil, and oregano.

Basics of the Mediterranean Diet Plan

The basis of the diet calls for plant foods which moderately low in animal foodstuffs. On the flip side, it is advisable to consume fish or seafood for at least two days of the week. You will want to consume plenty of water, and as previously mentioned; one glass of red wine daily is admissible. Tea and coffee are okay, but you should avoid sweeteners.

What You Should Eat

- *Dairy*: Greek yogurt, cheese, yogurt
- *Eggs*: Duck, chicken, quail
- *Healthy Fats*: Olives, extra-virgin olive oil, avocado oil, and avocados
- *Poultry*: Turkey, duck, chicken

- *Whole Grains*: Brown rice, whole oats, barley, rye, whole wheat, buckwheat, corn, whole grain pasta, and whole grain bread, etc.
- *Spices and Herbs*: Cinnamon, garlic, mint, basil, sage, rosemary, pepper, nutmeg, etc.
- *Seafood and Fish*: Tuna, salmon, trout, sardines, shrimp mackerel, oysters, shrimp, crab, clams, mussels, etc.
- *Vegetables*: Kale, broccoli, tomatoes, carrots, cauliflower, spinach, onions, cucumbers, Brussels sprouts
- *Legumes*: Lentils, peas, beans, chickpeas, peanuts, pulses, etc.
- *Tubers*: Sweet potatoes, potatoes, yams, turnips, etc.
- *Fruits:* Dates, grapes, strawberries, oranges, apples, bananas, pears, peaches, melons, etc.
- *Seeds and Nuts*: Macadamia nuts, cashews, almonds, walnuts, pumpkin seeds, hazelnuts, sunflower seeds, etc.

Note: Many of the Mediterranean Diet recipes call for olive oil; you will use the extra virgin type if it is not specified.

What to Eat in Moderation

- *Poultry*
- *Eggs*
- *Cheese*
- *Yogurt*

Rarely Eat: *Red Meat*

Avoid These Foods

- *Added Sugars*: Ice cream, candy, soda, table sugar

- *Sugar-Sweetened Beverages:* Avoid juices high in sugar

- *Refined Grains*: Pasta made with refined wheat, white bread

- *Processed Meat*: Hot dogs, processed sausages, etc.

- *Higher Processed Foods:* Any foods marked 'diet,' 'low-fat,' or factory produced

- *Trans fats*: Margarine and other processed foods

- *Refined Oils:* Canola, cottonseed, soybean, and others

Chapter 2: Breakfast Recipes

Almond Biscotti

Enjoy this to dip in your tea, cappuccino, or coffee.

Ingredients

1 pound flour

1 pound lightly toasted whole almonds

4 (+) 1 eggs

2 teaspoons vanilla

Zest of 2 lemons

1 teaspoon baking powder

½ pound sugar

Instructions

1) Preset the oven temperature to 350°F.
2) Prepare a cookie sheet with parchment paper.
3) Slice the almonds into halves.

4) Mix four of the eggs and the remainder of ingredients in a large mixing bowl.
5) Process the dough into a 1 ½-inch thickness making three logs. Place on the prepared baking sheet.
6) Beat and spread the last egg over the logs and bake for 30 minutes.
7) When it is ready, cut the logs into ½-inch wide slices.
8) Place it back in the oven at 300°F for 25 more minutes.

Breakfast Couscous

Ingredients

1 cup uncooked whole-wheat couscous

3 cups low-fat 1% milk

½ cup dried currants

1 (2-inch) cinnamon stick

½ cup dried apricots

¼ teaspoon salt

6 teaspoons (divided) dark brown sugar

4 teaspoons (divided) melted butter

Instructions

1) Using a medium-high burner on the stovetop; place a large saucepan and add the cinnamon stick and milk. Heat it until you see bubble formations along the edges. (Do not bring to a boil.)

2) Take the pan off the burner and blend in the apricots, couscous, salt, currants, and four teaspoons of the brown sugar.

3) Place a lid on the pan and let it rest for 15 minutes. Take the top off and throw away the cinnamon stick.

Serve the tasty meal evenly in four bowls and garnish with ½ teaspoon of brown sugar and a teaspoon of melted butter.

Yields: Four Servings

Banana Nut Oatmeal

Ingredients

2 tablespoons chopped walnuts

¼ cup quick cooking oats

1 teaspoon flax seeds

3 tablespoons honey

½ cup skim milk

1 peeled banana

Instructions

1) Mix everything together in a microwave-safe dish, except for the banana.
2) Cook two minutes on high.
3) Use a fork to mash and stir in the banana.

Serve piping hot!

Mediterranean Breakfast Quinoa

Ingredients

1 cup quinoa

¼ cup chopped raw almonds

5 dried apricots

1 t. ground cinnamon

2 dried pitted dates

2 Tbsp. honey

1 t. sea salt

2 cups milk

1 t. vanilla extract

Instructions

1) Finely chop the dates and apricots.

2) Using medium heat, toast the almonds three to five minutes in a skillet. Set to the side.

3) Heat the quinoa, salt, and cinnamon using medium heat until warm. Pour in the milk.

4) When the mixture boils, lower the heat, and place a lid on the pan, continue cooking slowly for approximately 15 minutes.

5) Pour in the honey, vanilla, apricots, dates, and ½ of the almonds.

6) Garnish with the rest of the almonds for a tasty treat.

Mediterranean Slices

Ingredients

85 g cheddar/grated or 125 g ball mozzarella cheese

375 g package ready-rolled puff pastry

140 g. container each:

- Frozen artichokes (3 wedges per serving)
- Sliced roasted peppers

4 tablespoons green pesto

Instructions

1) Set the oven temperature to approximately 395°F/200°C.

2) Unroll and cut the pastries into four rectangles (some may be pre-cut).

3) Spread one tablespoon of the pesto onto each of the four rectangles.

4) Add the artichokes and peppers.

5) Cook the slices for fifteen minutes in the preheated oven or just until the pastry begins turning brown.

6) Take the pan out and tear off the mozzarella ball into small bits, over the veggies.

7) Place it back into the oven and continue baking for another five to seven minutes.

8) Serve with a fresh green salad.

Chapter 3: Lunch Recipes

These are a few of the ways you can make lunchtime healthy and tasty!

Garden Wraps

Ingredients

1 cup Greek yogurt

2 tomatoes

1 tablespoon chopped each:

- Cilantro
- Chives
- Fresh mint

½ teaspoon kosher salt

½ cup each:

- Cooked peas
- Sliced red onion

1 ½ cups each:

- Sliced cucumber
- Shredded carrots

4 sheets lavash

½ teaspoon kosher salt

Instructions

1) Cut the tomatoes in half – slicing them thin.
2) Mix the salt, yogurt, and herbs in a small dish.
3) In another medium dish, mix the cucumber, carrots, cooked peas, and red onion.
4) Place one lavash sheet on countertop or platter, and add approximately ¼ of the mix of yogurt down the center, a layer of tomatoes, ¼ carrot mix, and fold/roll to one side of the flatbread.
5) Use several toothpicks to secure the ends. Cut it in half and repeat with the remainder of the products.

Note: Lavash is a Mediterranean soft flatbread.

Yields: Four Servings

Creamy Paninis

Ingredients

8 slices whole grain bread or ½-inch thickness

½ cup (divided) mayonnaise with olive oil

1/4 cup basil leaves (fresh is preferred)

7-ounces roasted red peppers (1 jar)

2 tablespoons chopped black olives

1 small thinly sliced zucchini

4 slices provolone cheese

Instructions

1) Finely chop the basil leaves.

2) In a small dish, mix the finely chopped olives with the mayonnaise.

3) Spread it on the slices of bread with the peppers, zucchini, and provolone. Top with the remainder of the slices.

4) Place mayonnaise on the outside of each sandwich.

5) On the stovetop using medium heat, place the sandwiches on a grill pan or skillet. Brown each of the sandwiches approximately four minutes.

6) What a treat with all of that melted cheese!

Yields: Four Servings

Broad Bean and Feta Cheese Toasts

Ingredients

4 thin slices baguette (brown or white)

350 broad bean (frozen or fresh)

1 tablespoon olive oil

2 tablespoons mint leaves

50 g bag mixed leaf salad

1 teaspoon lemon juice

10 halved cherry tomatoes

100 g feta cheese/drained/vegetarian alternative

Instructions

1) Prepare a saucepan of boiling water, toss in the beans, returning to a boil, and continue cooking for around four minutes.
2) Run cold water over the beans using a colander. Drain.
3) Remove each of the beans from the skins, and set aside in a dish.
4) Mix the mint leaves and crumbled feta, toss well, and flavor with two tablespoons of the olive oil and a sprinkle of pepper. Blend again with the tomatoes and salad leaves with the lemon juice and balance of the oil.
5) Divide this into two serving dishes.
6) Toast the bread on both sides.
7) Spoon the cheese and bean mixture on the toast next to the salad.

Chapter 4: Dinner Recipes

Lemon-Zaatar-Grilled Chicken

Ingredients

4 (6 to 8-ounces each) chicken thighs

1 teaspoon lemon zest

1 lemon cut into 4 wedges

2 tablespoons lemon juice

8 green onions

1 teaspoon minced garlic

¼ teaspoon each pepper and salt

Instructions

1) Blend the zest, oil, lemon juice, zaatar, pepper, garlic, and salt in a big container. Put the thighs into the mix and fully cover the surfaces.

2) Use a medium grill temperature setting ranging between 350°F to 450°F. Place the chicken on the surface—skin side down—for five to eight minutes.

3) Flip the thighs and cook for approximately four additional minutes.

4) For the last few minutes, grill the onions and lemon wedges—flipping once.

Note: The zaatar for this recipe can be located in the Middle Eastern section of most superstores.

Chickpea Patties

Ingredients

½ cup flat-leaf fresh parsley

1 can chickpeas (15.5-ounces)

¼ teaspoon cumin

1 garlic clove

1 whisked egg

½ teaspoon (divided) each:

- Kosher salt
- Black pepper

½ cup low-fat Greek-style yogurt

4 tablespoons (divided) all-purpose flour

2 tablespoons oil

8 cups mixed salad greens

3 tablespoons lemon juice

1 small red onion

1 cup grape tomatoes

Optional: Pita chips

Instructions

1) Preheat some oil in a skillet.

2) Rinse and drain the chickpeas. Chop the garlic clove, cut the tomatoes in half, and slice the red onion thin.

3) Use a food processor to pulse the first four ingredients (through the garlic clove), and add ¼ teaspoon each of the pepper and salt until the mixture is chopped coarsely and holds form.

4) Place the mixture in a bowl; blend the egg and two tablespoons of the flour.

5) Make ½-inch patties.

6) Roll the patties in the remainder of the flour.

7) Use med-hi heat and place the patties into the prepared pan, and cook them for two to three minutes for each side.

8) Whip together the lemon juice, yogurt, and rest of the pepper, and salt.

9) Divide the onions, greens, tomatoes, and patties and sprinkle with about 2 tablespoons of the dressing over each of the salads.

10) Add pita chips on the side.

Yields: Four Servings: Two Patties for Each Serving

Herbed Mashed Potatoes with Greek Yogurt

Ingredients

4 pounds yellow potatoes

1 cup Greek yogurt (whole milk)

¼ teaspoon pepper

2 teaspoons kosher salt (divided – more or less)

1/3 cup each chopped:

- Chives
- Dill
- Parsley

3 tablespoons softened butter (divided)

1 cup warm milk

Toppings:

2 tablespoons each chopped:

- Dill
- Chives
- parsley

Instructions

1) Yukon gold (thin-skinned) potatoes were used in this recipe; begin by peeling and cutting them into one-inch chunks.

2) Place enough water and one tsp. of salt into a soup pot or similar pot to cover the potatoes. Let the potatoes boil using the high heat setting. Lower to the medium setting, and boil about 15 minutes.

3) Turn off the burner, drain the potatoes, and place them back into the pot.

4) Combine 1/2 teaspoon salt, the yogurt, and 1/3 each of the dill, parsley, and chives. Set to the side.

5) Break up the hot potatoes with a potato masher.

6) Combine 2 tablespoons of butter, milk, the pepper, and ½ teaspoon salt. Mash the potatoes until fluffy.

7) Blend the yogurt into the potatoes.

8) Add to the serving dish, and garnish with the butter that remains, with the chopped herbs.

Notes for Leftovers or Make them Ahead: Before you place the yogurt into the potatoes; you can chill the potatoes for up to one day. Reheat until they are hot. If they are stiff, add a small amount of milk until you reach the desired consistency.

Yields: Ten to Twelve Servings

Chapter 5: Continue the Plan

You now have some of the information necessary to get your health back in line and feel better during the process. This chapter will provide you with some basic guidelines that will be useful for your continued success with the Mediterranean diet plan. Try out some of the tempting recipes for breakfast, lunch, and dinner.

Sample Meal Plan

You have got the basis for your meal plan; these will assist you on the days when you aren't sure what you want to have on the menu for the day.

Monday

A veggie omelet with onions and tomatoes and a piece of fruit

A whole grain sandwich with cheese; fresh veggies on the side

Mediterranean Lasagna

Tuesday

Oatmeal with raisins

Tuna salad

Salad with olives, tomatoes, and feta cheese

Wednesday

Oatmeal with nuts and raisins with an apple

Who grain sandwich with veggies

Mediterranean pizza made from whole wheat garnished with cheese, olives, and other veggies

Thursday

Eggs and veggies fried in olive oil

Greek yogurt with nuts, oats, and strawberries

Grilled lamb with baked potato and a salad

Friday

Omelet with olives and vegetables

Pizza

Grilled chicken with potatoes and veggies; fruit for dessert

Saturday

Greek yogurt with oats and strawberries

Veggies with a whole grain sandwich

Tuna salad and a piece of fruit

Sunday

Yogurt with nuts and sliced fruits

Leftover *Lemon-Zaatar-Grilled Chicken* from the night before

Broiled salmon with veggies and brown rice

Healthy Snacks

- Leftovers from dinner
- A piece of fruit

- Splurge/Apple slices with almond butter
- Berries or grapes
- Greek yogurt
- A handful of nuts
- Carrots

How to Eat Out and Remain on the Diet

1) Have seafood or fish as your main dish.
2) Request your food be cooked using extra-virgin olive oil.
3) Eat only whole grain bread with olive oil. Do not use butter.

The Substitution List

This is a short list of ways to help maintain your diet as a general outline:

- Instead of crackers, pretzels, chips, and ranch dip; try some celery, carrots, broccoli and salsa.
- Leave the white rice and stir-fried meat behind and replace it with some quinoa with stir-fried veggies.
- So, you really want that big dish of ice cream; leave it and have some pudding made with skim or whole milk.

Myths about the Plan

Myth #1: The Mediterranean diet is just another food plan.

Fact #1: The Mediterranean diet is a good food plan, but the plan helps in many other ways. The food is made to be enjoyed in a relaxed atmosphere which is equally important to your health as to what is on your plate

Myth #2: Have a huge bowl of pasta and bread; it's the Mediterranean way!

Fact #2: Pasta is usually a side dish with the Mediterranean culture; they do not eat like the Americans. The helping is generally a portion of ½-cup to 1-cup. Most of the meal consists of fish, vegetables, and salads; sometimes—a slice of bread or some grass-fed meat.

Myth #3: It is expensive to eat using this plan.

Fact #3: The Mediterranean plan is not expensive if you are making the creation from lentils and beans for the protein source. You are also sticking with the whole grains and mostly plants which are much cheaper than the processed or prepackaged food items.

Myth #4: Four glasses of wine are great since one is good for your heart.

Fact #4: The diet plan allows some red wines in moderation which means two for men and one drink for women daily. Over those limits, can be damaging for your heart, health, and well-being.

www.ingramcontent.com/pod-product-compliance
Lightning Source LLC
LaVergne TN
LVHW010333070526
838199LV00065B/5730